FACE TO FACE WITH
SHARKS

by David Doubilet and Jennifer Hayes

NATIONAL GEOGRAPHIC
WASHINGTON, D.C.

SCHOLASTIC INC.

New York Toronto London Auckland Sydney
Mexico City New Delhi Hong Kong Buenos Aires

David with his camera after photographing great white sharks. Shark cages have metal bars that are wide enough for cameras to fit in but close enough to protect us.

FACE TO FACE

A 16-foot-long great white shark bites our steel shark cage near Dangerous Reef, South Australia. A white shark can open its mouth wide enough to swallow a whole seal or a human.

We like sharks. My partner and co-author David and I spend many days a year in the water. We photograph all kinds of sea life and shipwrecks, but sharks are our favorite subject. David saw his first shark when he was 13 years old. The sandbar shark was bigger than he was! He was scared, but he still took a picture of it. I saw my first shark when a fisherman caught a big hammerhead nearby. When he cut it open, 20 perfectly formed baby sharks were inside of her. I was sad that the pups would not

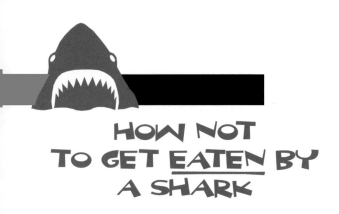

HOW NOT TO GET EATEN BY A SHARK

Very few people are attacked by sharks each year. But sometimes sharks do attack, so here are some tips on how not to get eaten by one:

— Do not swim where people are fishing or dumping bloody fish guts into the sea. Sharks may mistake you for a fish.

— If you cut yourself and you are bleeding, get out of the water.

— Do not swim at dawn or dusk.

— Always swim with other people nearby.

— Never touch a shark!

survive. Right then, I knew I wanted to learn more about sharks and decided that one day I would go to school to study them.

We have photographed hundreds of sharks around the world. Different shark species have different personalities. Sand tiger sharks are calm, and we can swim with them. Great white sharks are very fast, aggressive predators, so we photograph them from a special shark cage. We are always excited to see a shark while we are diving, but we are always careful and cautious because we are visitors in their world.

We have never been bitten by a shark. However, some sharks try to bite our camera strobe lights. The sharks sense the batteries' electric charge, and they think the strobes are alive and might taste good.

You never know when you will discover a shark surprise. One day we were swimming in eight-foot-deep water off the coast of Tasmania, a large island south of Australia. We looked down and saw more than 15 sawsharks with long snouts, called rostrums, hiding in green algae. We were shocked to see them there because sawsharks usually live in over 100 feet of water. These female sharks may have come into shallow water to birth their pups.

We had our favorite shark dive on a very calm day off Gansbaai, South Africa. We got in our round metal cage and went in. Right away, a 15-foot great white swam out of the gloom and smashed our cage hard enough to knock us down. She came back to the cage again and again, showing us her razor-sharp teeth and a mouth that could swallow us whole. More and more great whites appeared out of nowhere. Four sharks circled our cage at the same time. We stayed in the cage until the sun went down, even though we were cold. That day, 17 different great white sharks came to check us out. It was the best day ever!

⬆ *Shark expert Mark Addison named this tiger shark Barbara Ann. She and many other tiger sharks migrate to Aliwal Shoal off South Africa every year. Tiger sharks have beautiful stripes, but like tigers, they can be aggressive and unpredictable.*

MEET THE SHARK

Sharks are fish without bones. Their skeletons are made of flexible cartilage, like our noses and ears. They are good hunters, twisting and turning like underwater jet fighters. Sharks have been on Earth for 400 million years, surviving mass extinctions, ice ages, and hungry dinosaurs.

It is easy to spot a male shark. Males have two long, tube-like organs, called claspers, that hang under their bodies. Males use the claspers to fertilize the female's eggs.

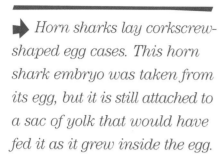
➤ *Horn sharks lay corkscrew-shaped egg cases. This horn shark embryo was taken from its egg, but it is still attached to a sac of yolk that would have fed it as it grew inside the egg.*

➤ *Adult horn sharks have pig-like snouts and flat teeth that grind up urchins and shellfish. Sharp spines next to their dorsal fins protect them from predators. Females lay a pair of eggs every 11 to 14 days for about four months. They can lay up to 24 eggs in one season!*

Some sharks lay eggs in the sea, but most give birth to a litter of live babies, called pups. Pregnancy can last from eight months to two years. Most sharks have litters of 10 to 40 pups, but the sand tiger shark has only 2 pups. The blue shark can have over 135 pups at a time, but few survive.

Sharks can smell blood and feel the vibrations

of a struggling fish hundreds of yards away. They also have a secret weapon called electroreception. They feel the faint electrical field that surrounds all living things. If we could blindfold a hammerhead shark, it could still find a stingray buried in the sand by sensing the ray's weak electrical signal.

Most sharks have good eyesight. They are very sensitive to light, and they can see better in the dark than we do. Great white sharks have poked their heads out of the water and looked right at us in our boat. They can see above and below water, just like we can. Some sharks even have a special eyelid called the nictitating membrane that slides

▼ *This lemon shark has just given birth in the warm shallow waters of the Bahamas. The pup is still attached to the mother by a placental cord. The cord will stretch and break, and the pup will swim into nearby mangroves for protection from other predators.*

▲ *A scientist examines the tiny razor teeth of a cookie cutter shark caught 3,000 feet below the surface in Suruga Bay, Japan. At right, this dolphin fish in the Bahamas has a perfectly round bite from a cookie cutter shark.*

across the eye to protect it when they attack prey.

Sharks can't chew, but they still eat everything in the sea, from shrimp to small whales. They bite, shake their heads, and tear away chunks of flesh. Biting is hard business, and their teeth fall out all the time. But you will never see a toothless shark, because they never run out of teeth. They have rows of new teeth ready to take their place.

Different kinds of sharks have different kinds of

A great white shark attacked this cape fur seal in False Bay, South Africa. The wounded seal swam into shallow water and died.

SKIN OF THEIR TEETH

Shark skin is a collection of tiny "skin teeth" known as dermal denticles. Each denticle has a tiny spike that points backward toward the tail. The denticles create a slip stream around the shark that lets it swim quickly and quietly.

■ Going for the gold: Some swimmers wear swimsuits that are designed like shark skin. The suits help reduce drag, increase speed, and win medals.

■ Like teeth, a shark's denticles are constantly lost and replaced throughout its life.

teeth. Some have flat plates for crushing food. Others have curved teeth for holding slippery fish or pointed, razor-sharp teeth for slicing and tearing. A deepwater shark called the cookie cutter has the oddest bite of all. This little 20-inch-long (50 cm) shark uses its thick lips to attach itself like a suction cup to a large fish, whale, or dolphin. It spins itself around, using a row of saw-like teeth to cut out a round "cookie" of flesh.

A Caribbean reef shark rests on the bottom of a cave. Many sharks must keep swimming in order to breathe, but some can lie still for long periods of time.

WORLD OF SHARKS

This 10-foot scalloped hammerhead shark was caught on a longline and set free. Their unusual heads and special vertebrae help them turn sharply. They often form large schools of over 100 sharks that swim together.

Sharks live everywhere in the ocean. They live in the frozen Arctic and in warm tropical lagoons. They live in the deep sea and in ankle-deep water. Some sharks, like the bull shark, can live in freshwater. In scary movies, sharks are sleek killing machines, but real sharks come in all sorts of wild and crazy shapes and sizes. They can be guitar shaped, cigar shaped, or flat as a pancake. They can be prickly or silky smooth, hammer-headed or pig faced, the size of your hand or as big as a bus.

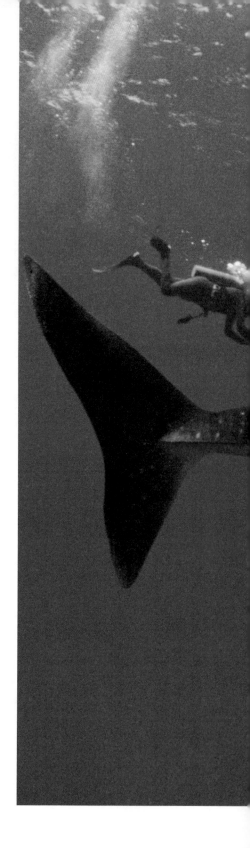

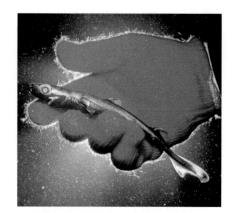

➡ *A scientist holds a dwarf lantern shark, one of the smallest sharks in the world. Whale sharks are the world's largest sharks. The 40-foot-long whale shark at right was part of a large gathering off Ningaloo Reef in Australia.*

Experts who study sharks and other fish are called ichthyologists. They have described about 400 species of sharks, but the ocean is a big place, and new ones are still being found. One exciting recent shark discovery is megamouth, a secretive 15-foot (5-meter) deepwater shark that takes in seawater and strains food from it. Scientists have also found a two-foot-long (60-cm) catshark that uses its fins to walk across the seafloor. They call it the "walking shark."

The smallest sharks in the world live in the deepest parts of the sea. Cigar-sized sharks, like the dwarf lantern and pygmy shark, feed on shrimp and squid nearly a mile down. The whale shark is the biggest shark in the world. It can be more than 40 feet (12 meters) long. The second-largest shark, the basking shark, grows to over 30 feet (9 meters) long. These

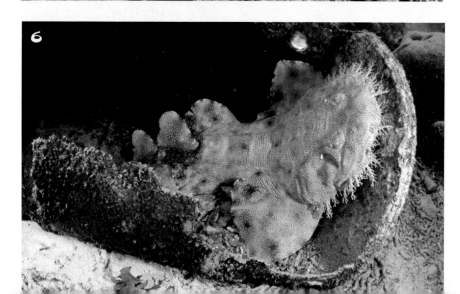

⬆ *There are over 400 shark species in all sizes and shapes. 1. Megamouth is a deepwater filter feeder. 2. Oceanic white tip sharks are open-water predators. 3. The foot-long puffadder shark curls up like a cat. 4. Elephant sharks dig in the soft sea bottom with their trunk-like snouts. 5. The epaulette, or "walking shark," uses its pectoral fins like feet to walk across the seafloor. 6. A wobbegong shark awaits prey in an old oil drum. 7. Sawsharks use their long snouts to search for prey.*

harmless, slow-moving filter feeders open their huge mouths and strain thousands of tons of water an hour to get to the tiny organisms called plankton.

The great white shark is one of the world's scariest predators. They mainly eat large fish, rays, and marine mammals like seals, sea lions, and dolphins. A few have attacked surfers. Still, they are not the fastest sharks—that's the mako shark, which can swim up to 30 miles per hour (48 kph) and can leap 20 feet (7 meters) in the air. The oceanic white tip shark is another fierce predator that lives off-shore. Closer to shore, tiger and bull sharks patrol the shallow waters. They eat everything from sea turtles to birds. Sometimes, they attack humans.

Not all sharks hunt big prey. The puffadder shyshark curls up like a cat when it's threatened. Horn sharks, sometimes called pig sharks, have no sharp teeth. They use hard plates in their mouths to crush shellfish. The sawshark uses its long rostrum to sweep through the soft sea bottom looking for prey. The wobbegong shark is a slow-moving carpet shark that looks like a bath mat. But watch out! They may look like they're sleeping when they're not. They're quick, and their curved teeth don't let go.

This fistful of fins in a Tokyo fish market will end up as an expensive bowl of shark fin soup. Millions of sharks a year are killed just for their fins.

CONSERVATION

A large school of Caribbean reef sharks gathers under our dive boat in Nassau, Bahamas. The Bahamas is one of the few places in the world that still has a healthy population of sharks.

Every year David and I see fewer sharks in the sea. We have spent the last five years diving on coral reefs in Indonesia, and we have not seen any large sharks. Many sharks and big fish such as grouper have disappeared from reefs all over the world. Where have all the sharks gone?

Humans kill more than 100 million sharks every year. Most sharks are caught and killed on purpose for sport or food. Fishermen catch them on long-lines (long commercial fishing lines with hundreds

→ *A row of dead porbeagle sharks for sale at a Tokyo fish market. Porbeagle sharks are listed as "vulnerable to extinction" because they live a long time, mature late, and have only four pups a year.*

CAN YOU SEE ME NOW?

Sharks are masters of disguise! Sometimes they seem to disappear right in front of us. This helps them sneak up on their prey.

— How do you hide the biggest fish in the world? Giant whale sharks are covered in bright white dots. The spots make them almost invisible in bright sunlight.

— Wobbegong sharks look like they are wearing a mask. They have fleshy fringe beards around their mouths that look and move just like waving seaweed.

of hooks) and in fishing nets. Sometimes the sharks are caught in nets set to catch other fish. This accidental catch is called bycatch.

Most countries do not regulate shark fishing. We have even seen unborn shark pups and 100-year-old whale sharks on Asian menus. Whale sharks are sometimes called tofu sharks because of their soft white flesh. Shark cartilage and liver oil are used for medicine and cosmetics.

Most sharks are killed for a bowl of soup. Shark fin soup is an expensive Chinese delicacy. Fishermen catch sharks, cut off their fins, and throw the

⬆ Shark expert Stuart Cove carefully feeds Caribbean reef sharks in the Bahamas. Thousands of people a year come here to dive and to learn about sharks.

sharks back into the sea, dead or alive. This is called shark finning. Without their fins, the sharks can't swim. They slowly sink to the bottom, where they can suffer for a long time before they suffocate or are eaten by other animals. Some countries have stopped shark finning, but shark fins are valuable. One pound of shark fin can sell for $300, and sets

23